Running the Voodoo Down

Jim McGarrah

Winner
Third Annual Elixir Press Book Awards

ELIXIR PRESS

Running the Voodoo Down

Elixir Press is a non-profit literary organization

Acknowledgments:
   Blesok (Shine): "Amber" and "Where Were You When I Needed You, Jack Kerouac"; *Cedar Hill Review*: "The Ballgame"; *Comstock Review*: "Thirty Years From the Tet Offensive" and "The Garden"; *Connecticut Review*: "Hearing the First Music," "Eating With Chopsticks in Vietnam," and "Joe's Elegies"; *Elixir*: "Self Portrait at Sunrise," "At the Museum of Modern Art," "Out of Focus," and "Running the Voodoo Down"; *North American Review*: "Black Ice" and "Generation Gap"; *Open 24 Hours*: "Absence," "The Art of Deep Breathing," "A Fisherman's Grace," "The Importance of My Baptism," "Snapshots," and "What a Man Really Needs"; *Pagitica*: "The Dentist's Office" and "A Note to Jill"; *Southern Indiana Review*: "The Memorial Wall."
   Special Thanks to Close Friends: Patty Aakhus, Ralph Angel, Matthew Graham, Richard Jackson, Jack Myers, Victoria Redel, Leslie Ullman, and Tom Wilhelmus. *Also*—RopeWalk Writers Retreat and Vermont College.

ISBN: 0-9709342-8-9

Author Photo: Jinx Halburnt
Cover Photo: Dana Curtis
Cover Design: Collin Hummel
Layout Design: R. F. Marsocci

Elixir Press
P. O. Box 18010
Minneapolis, MN 55418
www.elixirpress.com
info@elixirpress.com

Table of Contents

*This book is dedicated to the three people who allowed me to write it:
My wife Debbie, my daughter Leslie, and my son John*

Where is Nirvana?
Nirvana is here, nine times out of ten.
— Ho Huan Huong, *Spring-Watching*

Again, thanks for the dud
hand grenade tossed at my feet
outside Chu Lai. I'm still
falling through the silence.
— Yusef Komunyakaa, *Thanks*

Self Portrait at Sunrise

The woman at the café table across from mine scrubs
purple jelly from her boy's face. A blush rises
in its place and stains his skin. Monet saw daybreak
as the time without time when he painted
Impression: Sunrise, skimming and dipping
the brush through morning fog, fixing the movement
of light between sun and small skiff, touching
the silence of substance in the heart of form. Me?
I can't paint, not this morning or any other. Still,
when the boy's tears begin, days arc from my mind, flow
over the fan-shaped, cobbled square, and fade
into the brown labyrinth of Sienna, Italy, each day circled
by orange minutes that fracture into blue hours.
I've spent my life borrowing time from corpses.
"A picaresque hero," my friend Leslie says, "Who
lives as if his own breath is an unsolved mystery."
She's right. In this place, my self becomes undone
and leaves a myth like a hundred lire tip
for some waiter to sneer at. The boy sobs
as he lays his head on his mother's shoulder,
and so does she, reminding me that things I've always
been certain of—a fish cooked in milk is poison,
Deena didn't mean to swallow
my gum the first time we kissed,
love chatters like false teeth in cold water,
that shrapnel killed God, not Nietzsche,
thoughts as familiar and foreign
as the bullet fragments in my left leg—
don't stop the myth from crying. It comforts me,
is taller, more handsome, and the language
it speaks is less scarred. Years ago it saved
Bobby Wolfe from stepping on a land mine, pulled
Rick's rifle barrel away from his own chin before he jerked
the trigger, and never slit a Vietnamese throat

for refusing *chu hoi* in the jungle. The myth
has an appetite that knows no limits, never feels
alone in rooms full of people, and writes poems that never
ask why a man dies and the one beside him lives
through the same explosion of the mortar shell
every day for ten thousand nine hundred and fifty days.
It's legendary in liaisons with single women
and forgetful of its own failed marriages. It prophecies,
walking into the wilderness barefoot and bone-tired
in search of mystic stones. It's an angel
who brings the message to deaf generations,
a dragon that breathes the fire of empty wine kegs
into my mouth, a lover who dances naked
into the wild Tuscan night and ends up quietly watching
a boy and his mother share grape jelly with their tears.

Where Were You When
I Needed You, Jack Kerouac

Above me the stars tremble
like quartz flakes in a candle-lit cave.
My mind is silent
as it dreams, until
I swallow four tabs of No-Doz
with mescaline, then it screams
in colors while the Oldsmobile
sheds highway
like a blue snake escapes
old skin and begins again.
Turning right, turning left, turning
right into a labyrinth of tequila
and adobe homes, I'm switchbacked
by Pemex stations, cantinas, and mountains
that rise beside me in the salmon colored
smog of dawn. The more I learn
of language, the less I know of life
and loss. The asphalt melts
into a pearl beach, a ribbon of jet set
stores, juke joints, a KFC, and forlorn
taco stands. Acapulco, Mexico sings
a brown Coltrane song of concrete and sand,
discordance with purpose, clarity
in confusion. Cruise ship klaxons and car
horns blow the Deguelo of an all-night
mariachi band and produce markets of tanned
flesh call me toward Roceria.
Her tongue pours over my mind
like warm Kama Sutra oil and the quickening
of sunlight traps me in my own shadow.

That old black magic has me in its spell
That old black magic that you weave so well

5

J'ai L'ai rackets and bullfight posters,
Federales so young they still laugh,
grapefruits, bananas, mangoes, and grapes,
the smell of chili powder tied
in humid chords of air with café con leche
and cow dung, everything is real
including the nothing that hangs
on the tourist board outside Sandborn's
diner where I park the car.
I've driven all these miles and years for a note
from her and found this posted on the sterile cork:
"Michael call home."
"SWF needs ride to Baja—will party."
"Lost wallet found—empty."
"For sale, moped—slightly bent frame."

I can't dance don't ask me

What makes a single kiss
final one day and the next day leaves you feeling
as if the stove's left on and the whole meal's burning?

Roceria once told me that only Jack
Kerouac knew the secret of life and I said,
"What? Gallo Port wine in a glass of despair?"
She said, "All humans are really sharks," and climbed
aboard a crowded bus with her back to me,
her hair braided and swaying, a black metronome
of promise that has clicked through these past
years of memory and brought me back
to the Mexican beach where we met.
She must be fat by now with four kids
and a frequent black eye from her husband
as a badge of love. I must be crazy, still searching
for a goddess who was never more than human
and alone on a school holiday. I must be
that shark of Jack's, eating everything around me
and swimming constantly, just to stay alive.

Hearing the First Music

(for Harriet and Jim)

When I saw that the cut bank on the Connecticut River
had framed itself with graduated rocks
long before the first man had played music,
I listened to the river's xylophonic scale on the stones
and stared eye to eye with a brown hawk
between a floor of treetops and rafters made from clouds.

Then I scaled the long trail strung with blue spruce
and mountain vetch, each step
toward the crest lifting me through light,
pulling cross-hatched shadows through my chest,
and the music the shadows made on the green ferns
sounded like butterflies falling.

Above empty tobacco barns, cattle farms,
horse paths covered with shopping malls, I struggled
over pterosaurs etched in shale by the same water
that snapped their wings and swept their souls
into the river bed a million years before,
their shrieks crumbling downward with the sandstone.

Sitting on a rock to rest,
my sweat escaped from all the life below
and mingled with the mountain mist.
The weight of blood and bone climbed skyward
on the blue kite my father flew for me when I was ten.
I became a raindrop that would not fall again, even in the rain.

Montreal Winter
(for Wendy)

Language is what I sleep with
since you left, letters tying down
ropes of thought that moan
like mooring cables
along this ice-scarred lake front.
Words walk with me between the cars
and snowflakes into O'Grady's Pub.
We rent a pool table, wrap
our fingers around a crooked cue
and play your favorite game.
But, I don't feel the tingle
of their anticipation
along my radial nerve
as the cue ball spins.
Verbs don't dance
to Carly Simon's most famous song
on the worn jukebox, or drink O'Grady's
white wine, so cheap it doubles
for varnish remover. Nouns can't laugh
or cry as the numbered balls
all roll in different directions
and clear the green cloth that feels
as smooth as the inside of your left thigh
against the palm of my hand.

How Did Coltrane Know?

A recording of "Blue Trane" burns fluorescent holes
in my unlit room. How did he know which notes
to blow? Coltrane sucked night into his lungs
                    and exhaled.

Chain smoking and cross-legged
on the floor, I send pale blue puffs twirling
in the trill of his horn, feathers caught in the updraft
                    of a mountain moving.

Somewhere between melody and variations on a theme
a small boy appears, staggering against the March wind
beside his father who holds a kite string and by it is
                    connected to the sky.

How did Coltrane know only saxophones are immortal?
                    Even angels die.

                              The sax moans
like wind through wet wood,
one note in time.

                              Flying above
a tail of memories, the boy breaks
free. The kite spirals into

                              soft notes, skims
beneath veins of blue light circling
the willows and the reeds

disappearing
into the grave silence
that always follows jazz.

Ghost Pain

An old barstool stands
in the kitchen between the stove
and the counter. My father used to sit
there before dawn, read the Racing Form
in the yellow light of a bare bulb,
drink coffee, eat Bran flakes,
and wait for my mother
to scream
that whole last year before she died.
No one sits there anymore.
Four steel legs stain the floor
as if the tile were infected with rust.
I walk past each day feeling the way
John Gibson must have felt
after his leg was blown
off by a B-40 rocket round
in the '68 Tet Offensive. He lay
in the hospital bed next to mine and clawed
the empty sheet, begging for morphine.
The nurse always laughed.
"That's just *ghost pain*," she'd say
and boot him up with another 5 cc's.

Absence

I funneled them into single
lines at the roadblock on Highway One, patted
them down for rusty pistols, fuses
and trip wire that made this Tet
deadly for us milk-faced Marines who stepped
off the wrong trail at the right time; but all they owned
they carried
inside them, spitting out fragments
with chipped and broken slang. *Beaucoup*
mal. Dien cai dao. Beaucoup mal.

A brown and stunning girl
appeared in my hands, as if pulled from a hat
or sculpted from clay and light. She shook once
with fear and the taut spark
of her body jolted my cold circuits.
Then she was gone, running
south with a wave of refugees
toward the corrupt and declining China Sea.

The most beautiful girl I ever touched
ran from me.

She rushed past Buddhist monks,
past temple doorways curling with carved circles,
red dragons and snakes, past saffron
robes swirling in the wind that swallowed
the blanched light of dawn and lifted
the scent of nuoc mam,
urine and burned earth like incense
while Hue rose from the smoked horizon.

Tonight, as the wetness from a one-time lover
dries indifferently beneath
a fan overhead and I'm bored by the murmur
of her sleep, I drift back
to that roadblock and that strange girl's voice,
to her almond cheeks,
her thin lips, the slight white scar
beneath her left eyebrow,
to her hollow gaze and boyish breasts.
I feel her fingers, frail
yet resolute as a spider's web.
They wrap around my wrist, push
my whole being away.
I want to taste the red wonder
of her tongue, draw
those onyx eyes across ten thousand miles
of death and into me. Instead,
I reach for my pants, curse when my car keys rattle,
slip from this motel, and dream
of making love to her
with what's left of love inside me.

Hop Along
(for Tom)

Phil thinks Hopalong Cassidy might have been God
reincarnated. Considering his point, I follow
his back down Bourbon Street, parting a curtain of jasmine,
sewage, bacon, and stale beer with my drunken body.
"This is the funk of life and bad love," he says,

but it's all too vivid for me, the smells, the embroidery cut
across Phil's western jacket and his long silver hair flashing
rainbows in the neon night. I can't help but wonder
why I'm here. What if all those evenings forty years ago
when old Hoppy galloped over the black & white TV screen

had passed me by as mere amusement and I missed some
apocryphal sign, some real second coming, returning now
to testify around the next corner on Rue Saint Ann?
If Hoppy and God were the same cowboy
then the existential dread riding herd on this outlaw
New Orleans night would simply be *nothing*.

Whew. It's only a mime who stands there and terrifies me
with gestures of a man imprisoned in a world he can't feel.
"I was Hopalong's stunt double once," says Phil. "I rode Topper
right off a goddamn cliff, then drowned. We all look like someone else
and you get a lot of pussy when you're a stunt man."

There's no one I can blame for Phil's brilliance or his 3-D
Technicolor cowboy boots as we cross Saint Ann and stop on Chartres
to ask for a table in the courtyard of the Napoleon House.
The bartender relives the history of Campari and swears
it's like life, never bitter if you add enough gin
and mix lime with the soda water. "Who would name a bar for a ghost
unless the ghost was a famous cowboy?" asks Phil.

13

Who would? And, looking over my shoulder, I speculate where
a mime might get off pretending he knows the secret of life
is contained in a handful of air.

What a Man Really Needs

When I read a story called *What Men Really Need*
I remembered you, Rough River State Park, and one hawk
bobbing in air currents high above the cave
on the cut bank, untouched by a flushed sun as it
wrestled night for morsels of day, as we struggled
over the hash pipe I bought in DaNang the year before.
Smells of woodsmoke and Mavrodaphne wine
startled me when your hair brushed across my face.
All I could do was scream at the unconcerned hawk,
"Where is your shadow?" "What happened to your dreams?"
I wanted to be alone. I wanted a shot of Jim Beam,
sex without emotion, a line of coke, electro-shock therapy,
sleep without nightmares, a quick death.
Isn't a way to live inside himself what a man really needs?
I haven't seen you, Becky, in twenty-six years, but I'm still
screaming at that hawk, trying to hang on currents of cold air.

Amber

For a long time
I've wanted to write
a poem beyond
the usual metaphors
for dying
that described
those last few days
my mother spent alive
in some small place
that I could only get to
behind the black holes
in her eyes.
Instead, I'm sitting
in the Hilltop Tavern,
eating lunch, notebook open
and stained with gravy,
staring down a pile
of scooped and mashed potatoes
with a single word
on my mind—Amber.
No matter how many ways
I pull, stretch, bend, and twist
this word, I can't make it fit
into a sentence with death.
Amber is the color
of cold beer the waitress
places on my table, the kind
mom said I drank
too often before cocktail hour.
Butterscotch candy tasted amber
when I was four years old
and choking on it. She
snatched me from the kitchen
floor, held me by my legs,

and slapped my back hard,
returning the life she had
already given. The tiger lilies
in the last of her small garden,
most beautiful right before they die,
smell amber after the sun
has opened and fed them
the amber source of that death
like the tiny mosquito trapped,
a small black spot with legs
and blood and wings, frozen for eons
in prehistoric tree sap called amber.

Angels

"She paints angels fairly well," my friend Rick said, ignoring
the small lens through each black eye painted clear enough
for the light outside to enter and show me

what I almost missed here in Ljubljana with its statues
of dead Romans that stand guard at GAP boutiques,
with its blue-haired students staring westward and waiting

for a hero who moves time from past to future with no damage
to the present, with its old stones and new poets that drink
Union beer and write the city's flight from centuries of blood

on the backs of bar napkins, with its Russian scars that never slowed
the swirl of this artist's brush from traveling where it wanted
when it needed to go there. "Her name is Metka," Rick said.

"She paints angels while her husband writes his demons into books."
I've never seen her but I spent the day inside her, injecting
my memories like oil-based colors onto her canvas faces—

the blonde angel who wrapped her legs around my waist
while her sister shot me full of coke and cried
because I came before she had the strength to climb on,

the blind angel who dropped a hit of mescaline in a park, dancing
while Duane Allman played the blues, while she saw
a rainbow in the sky behind her frozen eyes, and that one freckled

angel with red hair whose skin was so soft that I forgot the pieces
of my best friend lying in the yellow mud of Khe Sahn and the stare
of a child who sat beside a dead dog, waiting for war to end.

I've lived a death suspended with angels just like hers,
framed by the sterile light in some small gallery on some narrow
street, the air aching between their eyes and mine.

The Art of Deep Breathing

Because I loved brushstrokes of blue air caressing the pink canvas
of my lungs I asked the supply sergeant for a rifle that worked.
Mine fired the first time and jammed. I was green, so he said, "No,
the Corps issues each jock strap one gun. Tough luck."
Outside the supply tent, I burned leeches off my left thigh.
The scent of Marlboros and scorched flesh sickened me. Thinking
of that fat sergeant, his two-beer ration, wrinkled Playboys,
    and warm tent,
I felt the cold night wind as it marched the rain along the Rockpile, down
from the DMZ. I hated how he stayed dry while I got wet.

Because I loved letters from Lynn Romer, molars grinding on cookies
mom mailed, pictures of sis in her prom dress, cheap perfume rising
from the half-French whore's neck, and a hot shower with real soap,
I asked the First Lieutenant to inspect my rifle. He squeezed
    off one round
at the Phu Bai rifle range. "Works fine boy. The problem's in your head."
"The casing won't eject, sir," I whined. "If I have to fire twice, I'm dead."
But he refused to listen. He said, "The first man up the hill's a hero."
I thought-the next one's a politician. From a foxhole,
    Armed Forces Radio
played Jimi—*Hey Joe, where you goin' with that gun in your hand*—.

Because I loved that swirl of orange flashing behind my eyes,
the adrenaline that embraced the art of deep breathing,
I took my broken rifle on patrol. I dreamed I saw one lieutenant
and one sergeant through my sights. At the right angle, a single shot
would do them both. Death by friendly fire is unavoidable in combat,
and no one questions a scared soldier with a broken rifle.
    Walking point, I
was an easy target filled with strange thoughts. If only I could have gotten
into a supply unit as an officer, I would be fat and fearless, breathing deep
and firing my rifle at nothing. I never wanted to kill anyone, anyway.
I just wanted to know I could.

The Importance of My Baptism

One hot Sunday in 1959, Grandma Bruner
hauled me to the county fairgrounds in the back
seat of her pea green, fluid drive, '48 Chrysler.

Once there I watched in awe as a grim man,
whose first name was Reverend, healed the sick
and revived the apathetic by reducing their silver content.
Reverend glowed with abstinence. A pink corona
floated from his cheeks. His gaze coaxed
a row of sweat from under a sinner's brow.
The beads danced and shook. The front pew trembled.

Reverend's voice railed against the stiff canvas air
in the revival tent. I wanted to be saved. I needed
salvation, grandma said. All boys twelve years old
walk with the devil—like when I shot my neighbor's cat
in the ass with my new Daisy air rifle or watched my sister's
best friend undress. Heal me Reverend. Hell
is no place to spend puberty. Praise God.

In an instant, the Spirit surged through my veins.
I felt lightheaded. I began to sway like a cobra
rising from a basket. The power of his holy words
addicted me. The organ ground out a melody.
The choir director rose and flailed the air while the choir
marched the lyrics, lemming like, off the stage.
It was my call to heaven, my doxology of destiny.

"Praise God from whom all blessings flow.
Praise Him all creatures here below."

"You are a creature from below," Grandma said
pushing me into the aisle toward baptism, past the tight buns
of housewife hair that made each frozen housewife glare.

The altar rose before me,
levitating on the Reverend's taut tongue.
"Eli, eli la' ma sa bach tha ni?"
I could feel the healing, like the lifting of a weight.
The audience felt it too as their pockets poured
into the offering plate.

"Praise God from whom all blessings flow.
Praise Him all creatures here below."

Two years after my baptism, God took the Reverend
to his new home—a satin lined box buried in black dirt.
"Are windows in there so the Reverend can see out?"
I asked my father at the graveside service.
"The only window into hell is between your ears," he said.
"Through that window pain is accomplished,
while the rest of the world eats dinner."

I learned what Dad meant
the first time I got laid, which was actually standing
beneath the eave of an old warehouse.
She smiled coldly, a tall girl with a flat chest
and hard-to-reach heart.
I was just another teenage ballplayer.

Her crisp voice called me into the shadows.
A tongue of moonlight licked through the clouds,
leaving a pale trail across bare thighs.

I felt my palms sweating,
fumbling for unfamiliar snaps, zippers, and images
underlined in a worn copy of *Tropic of Cancer*.

For a few seconds, I was king, commanding all women
to bow and kiss my scepter. I wanted this one girl
to genuflect in my presence forever.
Instead, she laughed and left me with five small words.
"Boy, that was quick, Squirt."

"Praise God from whom all blessings flow,
Praise him all creatures here below."

Black Ice

Those stories of an entire life
flashing by in seconds—lies—all the stories
are lies. What you remember when the black ice
on the black asphalt of Route 87 levitates
your car, offers it to the dead stars, and leaves you
confused between the air and wild rock face
of Upstate New York, what you remember

is the train station in Cuernavaca. You're standing
next to Roceria. The smell of diesel fuel,
roses, and vanilla tangles in your nose as her black jungle
of hair brushes goodbye across your face. What you think
about as the car bounces off the guardrail
and marches backward down the cliff to the cadence
of metal shredding, what you think about

is your last breakfast in Mexico, the way her tiny wrist
sprinkles chili powder over grapefruit
while the sunrise falls in red grains through the green trees.
You've never seen anyone do that before and you wonder
how the memory of spice can ripen
the memory of sweetness so much
that six thousand miles and thirty years later,
when the car finally stops spinning,
all you can taste as you bite through your lip
is the warm, metallic flow of regret.

Generation Gap

When the moon is full my son transforms
himself. He and his friends leave
white suburbia behind by simply driving
their Levis four inches down below the waist,
steering stocking caps over straight hair,
and playing rap songs through devices they mistakenly
call "sub-wolfers." Our neighbors, unaccustomed
to loud thumps accompanied by strings
of words that rhyme with *bitch, cock, gat,* and *clit,*
have called the cops four times.
"What makes you want to be someone you're not?"
I asked my son right before
shutting the circuit breaker to his room down
and chasing his friends out.
His lips made sounds like bees buzzing—ism—
ism—ism—ism—Schism my gism.
But, misplaced Ebonics won't answer the same question
I couldn't answer for myself on a spring night in '66.
After I throttled one recalcitrant burst of acne
into submission and wiped it away with Stridex,
after my parents handed me a set of vinyl luggage
and a bus ticket to some faraway private college
and after Mona refused to jack me off in the driver's seat
of my '57 Belair because she was left-handed, I walked
into darkness with that question, like plasma, pulsing
through my mind. Before the night ended my friends
and I stole a case of beer from the Humphrey's
back porch and drank till the stars exploded
in bursts of pepperoni pizza over Converse high tops.
We screamed "get fucked" at a State Trooper
as we sailed past the old refinery on Highway 41
in a '63 Dodge Charger borrowed from my father,
top-ended and almost sobered by the wind at 110 mph.
We swam the White River naked, each one daring

the others to go first. And I did, as if the habit of being led
had suddenly become my own desire and the distance
between this shore and that one might be measured
in breast strokes and ragged breath alone, without regard
for current, snags, or a tricky undertow. I wanted
to be someone else if only for a moment, to scream at the world
"You don't scare me" and show my friends
that slight tilt of the head, the arrogance
of young manhood that threatened to drown us all.

Cracked Glass

I once called this man friend, a beast of burden who
shared my fear of dying, bearing it beside me through

bamboo shoots, elephant grass, and brackish paddy water.
We burned leeches from our backs, wandered into the scream

of Phantom jets and the whine of burning jungle.
Motown music danced, little fireflies of sound, between

tracer rounds and the osmosis of flesh and earth and sky.
I could have kissed this man a hundred times and wanted to.

I wanted to give myself to the one person who might know
where I was going and wait for me till I got there.

Now, three decades later, I'm sitting at my desk
with a cheap, glass-lined thermos full of ice and good vodka,

meaning to share him with the world by breaking lines,
composing words into strange strophes of presence through absence.

Instead I pour a cup of cracked glass and learn what happens
when you mix strong drink and bitter cold inside a container

made to hold something hot. I can't remember my friend's name.

The Artist

Joe poured
a mound of Velvet onto paper
thin as a new blister.
The smell of solvent and sawdust
rose from the concrete floor,
he licked and lit the cigarette.
It disappeared, a mist of blue smoke
mingled with the exhaust of a crippled car
and the gray flesh of his grease-stained face.
He spoke, "Hand me that wrench boy."
Sunlight falling into oil and water braided gold
with blue and green as he jumped onto the fender
and attacked the broken crankshaft,
"Goddamn bolt's rusted."
"Was your dad a real Indian, Joe?"
"Cherokee, and this is all he taught me."
The engine, trembling, came undone
at the twisting of the wrench and exposed
its naked bearings to his soft touch.
When it was over, eight cylinders hummed
like whispers of leaves across the living earth.

I have an idea why Joe's been dead
these past twenty years,
though his whiskey riddled heart
got all the blame. He told me his dream once,
in simpler words than I remember,
the dream of painting winter wheat
as it roiled and bubbled, whipped
into rattle magic as the unseen spirit child
of sun and steam—of painting the trees
at the moment they formed forests, dawn
while it drained starlight from lakes,

autumn as it spun leaves into kaleidoscopes
of color, the motion of the river struggling
through the wetland as tribute
to his tribe that fished its banks three hundred years
before my father's father's father dammed its flow
to till the black bottom land.
Joe told me how hard it was to go on living in one life
when you belonged in another, like the man
he read about in the *Courier-Journal*
who went to bed speaking English and awoke
after a slight stroke, speaking words
he'd never heard. *Je suis perdu et seul.*

Today I'm standing in a mechanic's bay
looking at a boy named Bob plug sensors,
diodes, lasers, pulsars and several colored wires
into batteries, relays, resisters and injection ports.
Screens blip blue light. Bells ring. Buzzers buzz.
"You got a problem," says Bob.
"Can you fix it, Bob?"
"Well, that's another story. I'm no artist."

Dancer

Sheena rises
like a church spire
during her flaming star
dance at the county fair
this hot July night.
Her nipples swirl
higher and higher
till the flame bursts
from her breasts, looping
into the audience
with a sizzle and pop.
Farmers duck, young boys
giggle, and Reverend Swanson,
camouflaged
in tee-shirt and ball cap,
thrusts both hands
into starched overalls, as if
squeezing his long sad
sigh upward.

We all hurl silver coins onstage
till the fire falls, the music grinds
down, and I recall
a hot July
many years before.
I loved Sheena then,
when the image
of her bare breasts was firm
beneath my mother's sheets
and stroked me to sleep
that teenaged night I
first saw her.
Life seemed simpler then, sounded
like the rumble of straight pipes,

smelled of herbal shampoo
and baseball glove oil.
Nothing sagged,
not even my high school
batting average
or her eyelids heavy
with hemp.

This time it's different.
We face each other
with smiles that crack
the scars across our faces,
with stiffer gestures and slower
motion, with eyes glazed
in ceramic boredom,
with a need for balance
instead of grace.
I watch her nipples burn
in lethargic yellows,
blue heat banished
by the sense that what
we've both out stepped
for all these years
in the frenzied memory
of her dance has finally
run us both to ground.

Eating With Chopsticks in Vietnam

"L'homme est ne' libre."—Rousseau
"L'homme est ne' poltron"—Conrad

Eating with chopsticks was art not easily mastered,
or so I learned when the village elders led my squad
beneath the tiled roof of the old French schoolhouse
and fed us *cahn cho* in wooden bowls.
We rinsed it down with red rice wine in the noon
heat of the Lunar New Year
and I mastered the art before the meal ended.
Laughing, I balanced one grain
between those two sticks of wood while the air filled
with sweat and ginger, while the sniper steadied
his rifle in the fork of a rubber tree.
Marty pointed at my success, and babbled like a child who saw
the wonder in a rose petal for the first time before he dropped
face first into the scalding duck soup,
as if the sniper's bullet had pried open a small door
above his eyes, crawled in, and flicked the switch off.
In that split second I could have painted substance
within a shadow, written a book that breathed, sculpted
a living form from marble, or composed a score in silence.
I was supernatural, a Jeremiah in jungle boots who saw
the world's future between the rice on the wood and Marty's
blood and bone on my face like wet sand. Then I ran
for cover and hid behind a chipped stone wall.

Elegy for a Postal Worker

When you scrub china
in hot dishwater and remember
Brenda, it's not because
you ever saw
her in the kitchen
in the ten years you carried
mail together, stopping
for lunch at Metzger's Tavern
almost every day,
glasses clattering in the background,
while you both laughed
because your separate dreams of doing
great *things* had been reduced
to fried bologna sandwiches
and stuffing utility bills
in strangers' mailboxes.

So now, the clink of dishes
and the clatter of spoons,
the hiss of the faucet and the squeak
of the towel across clean glass,
the sounds you'd expect
her home to make if she were in it,
and the scent of her lilac
soap as it used to wash the air
on those mornings you hid
behind the convenience store,
remind you of who she was
by what she wasn't.

When the cancer hid in Brenda's breast
and nested there, she phoned.
What do you say
to someone who knows
she's dying and can't hide from it?

How do you hide from her funeral?
Maybe something comes up, a trip to the dentist,
a TV show, a new job offer, laundry,
the guilt from knowing that though you were older
and maybe less worthy, it would be you
and not her who sent flowers.

Mom Was the First American Practitioner of Feng Shui:

Like a sentry sitting on a barbed wire perimeter, she'd catnap through the howling dog next door, the clunk of our old air conditioner when the compressor kicked, the slam of sis's door, and the loud static of my worn 45's as Elvis stepped on Carl's *Blue Suede Shoes*. 1959 was not a quiet year in our home, but those sounds were all outgoing friendly fire to her. Like any good soldier, she responded to "incoming" every Tuesday at 12:15 AM. Fifteen minutes after the Elks Club closed, the light crunch of rubber tires echoed over our chat-covered driveway, a sound so slight that you thought a hundred small moths had flown into the bug zapper hanging in the garage, causing Mom to bolt upright in bed and sneak into the living room, carefully rearranging the recliner, the sofa, the coffee table, reading lamp, and rocking chair. Dad was home, drunk on gin and reeling from the loss on the last roll of snake eyes. It was inevitable in those Eisenhower days when the rest of the country got fat and sassy that he would end up broke and philosophical. "It's a long road that never turns," he'd mumble, the words just loud enough to filter through an open kitchen window, and then walk into the house. He always hit the sofa first, ricocheting from misplaced furniture to reeling wall like a bullet until he fell to the floor with a spent "Goddamn it." In the mornings, as Dad snored and the rest of the house awoke to the sizzle of bacon and the hiss of Folgers coffee mixed with the sweet scent of maple syrup and revenge, Mom shuffled all the pieces back in place and waited for Dad to get up.

The Horse Farm in Hot Springs, Arkansas
(in memory of Annie Burchell)

Shadows, the first gray shades
of aging light, sprint between fence posts.

Two fillies,
one bay and the other chestnut, outrace
dust swirls, outstep the flowing dusk.

I walk behind the sagging fence line
as if the posts, painted black and peeling,
might hold back the whine of passing time.
We built this pasture twenty years ago,
Bobby, Ann and I. Sweat and clover drifted
over our burned faces as calloused
hands chipped the shale hillside with a rusted pick
and set Ann's dream of breeding great horses
into the solid earth. The dream trembled
with each stroke of the ten pound sledge.

While I watch the fillies whirl, pawing playfully
at their outlines on the sun browned ground, Ann's
ghost fries fish atop the old stove in the farmhouse,
chain-smoking, mumbling of ways this place
could have grown into something more
than another home for mediocre thoroughbreds
if only she had given Bobby and me
her power to calculate
a vision from the sum of stud and mare.

I found her after breakfast on the barn floor
where she had gone to feed the yearlings. Black
oozed from the corner of her mouth and soaked the dirt
like the oil stain from the red Ford pickup beside her.
The surgeon said it was one of those things,
a freak accident, the kind impossible to explain.

I didn't believe him then, and still don't.
The dream killed Ann.
Its dappled coat and muscled flanks
lulled her into a quiet place
and she forgot the risk of reaching
for it from the dark corner
of an unbroken horse's stall. That dream kicked out
and drove itself through Anne's heart with the snap
of a shattered sternum and the sharp thrust of lost time.

Galloping a Dream

In this dream it is midnight. I tighten the girth
and gallop a chestnut mare along the racetrack rail.
The track is full of shadows inside the moonlit shadows.

She's skittish when the wind begins to rattle
fine sand across my face, as if guitar strings wailed
and snapped, as if shadows sang within the shadows

dissonant melodies, one note at a time, fractured
by my rapid breath against her neck and her own pale
hoof beats in between the moonlight and the shadows.

The night smells like fear, although
dreams have no scent until awakened with the detailed
stutter of hooves when she bolts the turn, jumps her shadow

and, with my waking, draws the reins to bow
her neck against the wildness of her dread. I flail
my knees against her flanks with false bravado,
think of whispers from my sleep and then I know,
"A horse can't outrun itself, but will always chase its shadow."

Out of Focus

In '69, I met a wild-haired man named Reggie
who walked an empty dog collar on a stiff leash,
who prowled the savage island between adolescence and adulthood,
popping Dexedrine, swilling Ripple, talking baby talk
to the dog collar. "Gude poochie. Poochie poochie hoochie coo."
Reggie was ill, contracting attention deficit from a whore
years before it became a medical disorder.
The first time I saw his paralyzed smile, we smoked black hash
laced with white veins of opium. Our feral eyes drifted with the smoke,
unmoored skiffs in a current of cold light.
I got a hard on when Reggie's girl rubbed her tiny tits
across my arm and asked for the last toke.
I passed the pipe, but Reggie stood there frowning
and sucking air as the water pipe bubbled.
The strange girl giggled "All gone." Reggie's right foot
pounded the pavement and he sang along with a
    John Lee Hooker 8 track,
"I'm your poochie poochie man. Everybody knows I am."
His voice squealed like sneakers on a clean gym floor.
When the tape ended, Reggie turned his collar up, petted the air,
and walked slowly into the night.
He's a chemist now, hired by Bristol Myers
because of his phenomenal pharmaceutical knowledge
and I'm a poet, drunk on words, stumbling over
the illusion of art.
For twenty-eight years we've brushed our wild hair away.
He helped develop Prozac too late to save his own brittle grin
or my last few healthy brain cells;
but the man still walks an empty dog collar late at night.
He just bought the John Lee Hooker box set on CD.
Some evenings we sit together on a park bench, smoking dope
until the moon changes colors and the dog collar pisses on my leg.

April 17th

A one-armed woman walks her golden retriever in the sunlight.
Two men patch mobile home windows with plywood. Casey's market

sells day old donuts, one dollar a dozen, and the coffee gets remade
while I wait for Casey to explain how beauty is nurtured by filth.

"Roses grow in horse shit," he says. The dog tugs at the leash, pulling
the woman off balance. Her leg rises and her shirtsleeve wraps

around behind her back as if she holds a baseball in a fist of air.
The stretch, the hesitation, the high kick of the left leg, the right arm

whipping forward and memory spins my best pitch off my first two
fingers toward childhood and the leathered face of grandpa

who always read the obituary in the morning news and if he didn't see
his name, ate breakfast. "What makes horse shit filthy" I ask, "or

roses beautiful?" The air percolates and the coffee pot pops
like the catcher's mitt dropping my fastball on April 17th, 1957.

Grandpa screamed *Horse Shit!* that one time when the ball rolled
into his rose bush and I chased it in, ripping red petals from the flowers

as the thorns bloodied my bare forearms. My father had pitched
in the Canadian League for two years, till World War II swallowed

his major-league dream in the sands of a Normandy beach.
But he played catch with me in grandpa's garden on this day in '57

and almost saved the roses from my shotgun arm and flowering ego,
and me from grandpa's Tourette-like string of epithets hurled

across the lawn. Almost. "Here's a fresh cup," says Casey. So, I drink
Casey's coffee and feel the morning chill thrown east as the woman

pitches forward onto the rising sun. Driving toward home, I wonder,
since we play catch every day, what I might tell my boy

when he asks what makes roses grow in our garden and why
his grandpa drinks gin so early in the morning.

Clotheslines

I don't see them much these days, not since Laundromats
& Sears credit cards & Master Charge & affordable Maytags.
America,
land of microchips
        fiber optics
        titanium alloys
        HD TV
        & space age plastic

                        has ceased to hang its laundry,
like my mother once did
on taut lines of hemp between the sag of an old chicken coup,
the glint of a gold Plymouth & the taste of those Eisenhower
decade dreams—2.5 perfect children & a quiet menopause.

I'm told that's a good thing, like a pay raise at Christmas,
or one of dad's sure winners at the track. But, I miss
the childhood smell of bleached light and soap woven
into fresh cut grass
& rinsed through the fabric
of an early May day.

My mother never seemed to tire
of reaching in her apron for those old wooden
clothespins, or chasing the sleeve of my father's white shirt
as it fluttered along the line in a fit.

The fatigue came later as I grew older, the language
vaguer with the miles between us, & whatever it was
that she had hoped for through me got frayed
around the edges of my acid trips, bad
marriages, lost jobs, & soiled visions, fading
with the wash of years over her face.

The Dentist's Office

It's peaceful somewhere between Mars and Venus
because there is no sound, and in space my nose
would never smell burnt flesh mixed with mint.
My mouth would swallow no blood, nor gag nor spit.

I'd be at peace somewhere between Mars and Venus,
because no young dental hygienists live there,
no breasts rest lightly on my forearm,
no perfect smiles encourage me to love my pain,
no perfume tingles in the deepest recesses of my groin
while my jaw goes numb and words of love
tumble out in drool soaked cotton.
"Iz if fafe? Iz if fafe?"

There's no peace on this planet
because humor is seductive only in space.
My best impression of Lawrence Olivier leaves
the hygienist unimpressed. She's too young
to recall the dentist scene in *Marathon Man*
and wants me to open wider as she scrapes
an aged nerve and leaves me to contemplate
the wild suck of the water pic if it slipped
from her hand and landed between my legs.

A Vietnam Veteran Visits Hemingway's House in Key West, Florida, circa 1971:

A human starfish trapped in white sand, I bought a ticket to your home just to cool off and found it filled with tour guides, scrubbed, sterilized, chanting hollow litanies of ex-wives and the search for one true sentence. Was this my salvation from myself, drifting from one mausoleum to the next, collecting memories like ashes and words like dead flowers? Inside each room your ghost, surrounded by faded French tapestries and photos of dead matadors, spoke of a time when souls were sucked from men in war and only words were left to fill the shell. I felt your presence where you wrote your stories surrounded by cats, staring down the barrel of a fountain pen the way Manolete stared over his muletta, daring a wounded bull one more pass. You counseled me like a Greek god, gun runner, rum smuggler, and master of whores, while I, Don Quixote in dungarees, vowed to become your reflection, tilting toward syllables unwritten and searching for ways to exorcise my own memories. I saw me as you must have seen you, hiding inside the belly of a book from the same rain, mud, napalm, and blood exploding on the same page of a different war. Once, I gathered pieces of a child's father and watched the child cry because the pieces didn't fit. Did you sleep with children's faces in your dreams? How hard was it to live as a legend? How hard was it just to live? Your war flowed into waterfalls of famous narrative until the language became your life and bled you dry in Idaho. I wanted to reflect your reflection through my own, but an imitation life soon wears like a cheap suit. From the Florida Keys I drove the Pan Am highway, drank Mezcal in Vera Cruz, puked peyote in Guadalajara, screwed whores, ran the bulls, and searched the alleyways and dirty bars of every neon city for the "one true sentence" that would erase the sounds of dying. I never got it right. I never mastered the art of impersonation. The lesson you taught me was one you left unlearned. No man can live forever as someone else, no matter how much he hates himself.

The Man Who Hotwalks Horses

When hay bales give birth
to hidden Smirnoff bottles, Red Harvey
is happy. Variations performed by vodka
off the theme of constantly walking
without thinking, cooling out thoroughbreds
fresh from their morning gallop, keep his
mind company. A bottle of cheap booze
playing hide and seek in clover
is more trustworthy than most people,
demanding only emptiness. Attached
to the horse's halter like a lifeline,
the leather lead shank is cracked and calloused,
flesh in his flesh.

Red sits outside the barn on cool autumn mornings
as dawn becomes a mist rising from the compost
and the air reeks of Bigel oil and bad coffee.
He waits for another horse that's lathered white
and snorting, and remembers
riding like a Cossack until the spill
at River Downs, breaking
his back. When the horse arrives, Red stands stiffly
and hooks the chain across its nose, moving like someone
whose mind is stricken with an uncontrollable question—
Has a man afraid to lose his life for his art
already lost them both?
and leads the horse into the shadows.

The Memorial Wall

1 – Arrival

You said Quang Tri was quiet when compared to Detroit
on Saturday night. I, being corn fed, believed you.
"Quiet as an old whore's bedroom," you said,
until the first whistle exploded and spilled
a mouthful of Tiger beer down my chin,
spraying the bolt on my new M-16. You grinned.

That smirk calmed all my fears
born in a place where ten seconds was a lifetime.
We lunged into a bunker when the next shell hit,
puppy clumsy. Like kids playing football,
chasing a fumble, we laughed, tumbling into darkness.

2 – Halfway Home

Rice wine burned us both, but opium seared the marrow
from your boyish conscience.
Disappointed, you asked why I'd fired too far left.
The kid was pulling up his pants, an easy target
in the twilight. He reminded me of a robin I'd shot
with my BB gun, squatting, pecking the wet ground
unaware of my existence, or its own thin mortality.
I was ten then and crying.

Your smile froze after six months in that country,
hiding a heart hardened by a dozen firefights
and memories sewn into body bags.
Those eyes, glistening with assurance,
connecting us as brothers, barely flickered
through Thai stick smoke and a Dexedrine haze.
Reeking of white phosphorus and cordite,
you swore that only housecats killed for pleasure.

3 – Short Time

It seems Monsoons came each day those last weeks
just to wash the blood away.
When our mortars hit the marketplace,
the barber's child died. Some stains
don't wash, like the memory of a sobbing man
whose only crime was cutting hair.

That's when I knew you were going home early.
The child's charred flesh made you unholy,
and the shortest distance from Vietnam to Detroit
was through blood atonement—your life for our sins.
When the shot popped, like a pricked balloon,
I realized you had fired it.
But, I screamed *SNIPER* to the corpsman,
so your parents could be telegrammed—*HERO*—stop.
Prying the rifle from your suicidal fingers, I thought,
you should have squeezed the trigger, not jerked it.
A clean headshot, instead of my right palm,
could have closed your eyes.

4 – Aftermath

We both flew home as casualties,
you in your coffin, me with my guilt.
You still deny me absolution
because you took the easy way back, Rick.
The dirt that covers your body now
fills my mind.
Each time I reach for some liturgy
to chant, some Eucharist to swallow
to understand your sacrifice, to bring sanity
inside the empty sound of a spring rain, I gag.

Here, in my kitchen, drinking cheap whiskey
like my mom sent us years ago in shoe boxes,
I grasp for some boundary.
If only I could leave you there in Washington, D.C.
on a black stone scarred with carved letters
and the tears of your children, unborn and unnamed.

The Covered Bridge in Wheeling, Indiana

Even the cross beams have rotted, their skeletons spliced
with young steel. Creosote covers the planks like chocolate

syrup, sticking to my boots. I trip over ill-fitted boards
in the floor and stop mid-way, listening to the creek roll

by below. The bridge moves with the water. I think
maybe the whole world is liquid, flowing toward the past

where hoofbeats echo and straw rustles through the corridor.
Spider webs of sunlight filter downward from the roof and trap

me by a scarred beam where two lovers etched a heart in 1905.
I feel their breath on the back of my neck as I trace its outline

in the wood. Oil and salt, sweated from their palms long ago, leaches
to my skin and rises in my blood until my own heart constricts

and I am old, like the bridge, held upright
by the grace of a cold current, pieced together by memory.

Replacing the Carpet

All night long I dozed lightly,
dazed and spun backward through time,
watching little orange meteors shoot
through my universe as if the roof
over my head had disintegrated
and I was a single blade of grass.

Now, in the dawn light, I remember
the Whitehouse Tavern. We got drunk
again and fought loudly.
I left you begging
in the dim neon light for one more
chance to stab my eyes
into their sockets with words.
I've don't recall what we argued about,
just that we did it with the elegance
and beauty of hungry animals.
Fred, your new lover, pushed his thumb
through the top of a salt shaker,
proving himself more worthy
of vicious affection,
but it was me you followed home.
I locked the door, forgetting you
still had a key, and played
something loud on the stereo till I fell asleep,

only to wake this morning and find the floor
at the foot of my bed littered
with your cigarette butts,
crumpled like fallen stars, bleeding
ash into the ruined carpet and leaving
your shadow to smolder in the fibers.

New Orleans Fais Do Do

Inside Poppy's Grill at 3:00 AM, the thin cook
steams burgers beneath a chrome hubcap.
The scent of sausage grease and cayenne pepper
reminds me that hunger, of one kind or another,
always quickens my pulse.

A dark man, blind with bourbon, staggers
from the stool at the end of the counter
to an old fashioned jukebox, presses L-7
and plays a Clifton Chenier song.
His ink-colored eyes find a boy, who's dressed
like Marilyn Monroe, in the corner booth.
Bon soir cher. Voulez-vous danser?

The cook flips a burger. The dazed boy rises, hesitates
like the drop of sweat on the cook's left temple,
and falls into outstretched arms, a blonde rose petal
that has rejoined the flower.

Politely, his calloused Cajun leads. Two as one
they spin, sputter, and tilt around the dining area.
I clap, nod, stomp my foot and try to stay in time
till the motion makes me dizzy. Swirling
from the heat of cheap merlot, my appetite
merges with the dance, the soft flow of air lifting
the skirt, the damp panic pressed between their palms,
the slide of worn leather on sawdust, and the hint
of salt that mingles with hot flesh when strange lips meet.

Getting Shot
(for Matthew)

When I recall the first time someone shot me
I think of Robbie with his BB gun, standing
in the apple orchard behind his aunt's house and aiming
at a small spot just left of my sternum. I turned
to run. The copper ball smacked the back of that spot
below my shoulder blade as if a wasp had flown
into my tee-shirt and, with cruel intentions, stung me.
Lying on the ground outside the orchard, I asked Robbie
if crying made me a sissy. "Yes," he said and died
two years later in a car wreck before he ever got laid.
Now it's morning, forty years later. The coffee
in this diner is weak. I'm glad. My stomach
sours easily as time slips backward and I lose my balance
in the haze between where my body sits and my mind dances
with the past. Out the window, I watch the Wabash River slide
through the fog around a bend and cut soil from the west bank,
one grain at a time. The silt disappears by becoming
the current, carried into shallows, swirled over snags, slapped
against the cheeks of stones that line the river bed until
a sand bar surfaces several hundred yards downstream.
When the first time I got shot flowed into the second, the pain
took the shape of bamboo shoots, rubber trees, and footprints
in the Monsoon mud, but it still smelled like rotted apples
and sounded like the hollow ping of Robbie's laughter.
In the jungle I asked the medic if screaming made me a coward.
"No," he said, "just a human who's a little further down the river."

Passing the Football

A breeze curls through empty bleachers
and limbs of a few oak trees with the echo
of shoulder pads cracking and whistles blowing.
The thunder of a hundred spikes
flays the dried earth in my mind as I pass
to my twelve year old son, whose flailing
arms rake the air and gather the football
over his right shoulder. I played
here long before his birth, struggling over
this patch of flat ground that seemed greater
than the sum of sweat, mud, and lime.

The game was tied at halftime
that last night of my final season.
Symbols clanged. Trombones
wailed a fight song while the bass
drum staggered the band back and forth
across the field the way the chipped
agitator in my mom's Maytag marched
dirty clothes. The soreness was beautiful
in the locker room, a butterfly rising
from the strains, sprains, and stretched groins
of taut boys shedding the cocoon
of childhood. Salt pills dripped
into my hand from a plastic vial mounted
on a wall that trembled when Coach
Reggie squealed, "Cunts. When you hit
a man, kill him. This is life. This is real."
We lost the game in the second half
and the cheerleaders' promises faded
to whispers in their frilled panties—Losers—
as they jumped and twirled the last cheer,
as the ref whistled us back where we started—
Incomplete.

Was it real when all you could feel
knocking dirt from your cleats was the rush
of rage up bruised legs and the distress
of a fat coach who hadn't won a game all season?
I thought so once before the plays became tactics,
the pads hung from my shoulders like flak jackets,
and whoever dropped the ball,
died. Now I want to scream—*incomplete*—
and start the play over. But the echo
is louder than the voice. My son charges
between the goalposts, dodges air, and dances
with the ball held high in both hands. He is king
of the end zone, champion on a field watered
with dreams instead of blood. The fire that burned
me burns blue in him, stoked by the hope
that the game goes on past boyhood and the rumble
he hears in his young veins will soon erupt.

Joe's Elegies—February 3, 2002

"The old lie: Dulce et decorum est, pro patria mori."
— Wilfred Owen

1. Agent Orange

In winter
the dead blow
where the wind goes:
through a cracked
window sill, beneath
an open coat collar around
a thick neck, behind
empty bleachers over
the football field, across
the Ohio river scarred
by the memory
of a speedboat's wake,
between the free weights
rattling at some brave
soul's out of season
yard sale, beneath the rising ping
of an engine with too many
miles and no warranty, the snap
of doubt in an all-weather American
flag and the strange cry of snow
spinning across a barren campus.

In winter
the wind blows
where the dead go,
shifting shadows into shapes
that terrify the living: a cemetery
of tulip stalks resurrected,
brought to attention and marched
at right angles to the ground,

shifting the weight of their dead
red helmets against the unbearable
burden of morning. Even the earth
can't hold the wind and keep it
quiet those first minutes
of dawn when it whines across
treetops and drops
the sun. Even the orange earth
trembles as the arc lights roar.

In winter
the wind belongs with the dead,
everywhere at once and nowhere at all.

2. VFW Post #1147

If I had backed my car from the garage this morning,
shifted to drive, aimed for Mrs. Taylor's Buick,
and pressed the accelerator to the floorboard,
then I would have been at war again because
war is my car wreck every day, seconds
slowing to hours as I close the hundred feet
between my bumper and her fender.
Metal crunching, glass flying, flesh ripping—
always good for mortality
checks and the illusion that soul is separate
from body. But I don't have the nerve for that kind
of action anymore. Instead, I drive
to the VFW, sit at the bar and wonder
when the seven rifles stacked
at attention in the wooden case might fire again. I wait
for the other old drunks to break ranks, stumble
from their stools, point the weapons skyward,
pierce the trumpeting of *Taps* with 21 sharp cracks
and the sweet smell of gunpowder.
In the end, dirt is all that gets shoveled over memories.
I think of Joe, those days we spent talking

about how Post Traumatic Stress Disorder was really
just the despair of living through the death of others,
and how I refused to ride in his speed boat
around the cut bank of the Ohio because
he piloted the Mekong thirty years ago, never
killing all the demons hidden in the tree lines
of his mind. I think of those last few words
he spoke to me before the Super Bowl came on
and he died, "Sometimes you know a brother
by the blood that runs through your veins,
and sometimes you know a brother by the blood
that runs out of them."

Note to Jill

I'm wearing the brown socks
you gave me.

They're beneath a table at the Mountainside Diner
waiting for me to half-eat half-cooked eggs
and wait, myself, for Rick.
He's the mechanic who swears
thirteen years of sobriety and promises
to fix my car, if he can just get the parts
from over the mountain before it snows, and if
those parts are the right parts, and if
State Farm Insurance mails the check, and if
his wife ever fixes him a warm meal, and if
his kids stop driving him crazy…

                                       Meanwhile,
Rick found me a nice room
in his brother's ski lodge (formerly the Route 9 Motel
before the repainting) at special non-skiing rates,
in case none of the above mentioned things occur this week.

The wall in my motel room (# 8) is thin,
like skin across the forehead that bleeds
profusely when hit with sharp objects, and for hours
my neighbors (# 7) throw
words against this membrane.
At 4 AM the screaming stops and the silence is terrifying.

That's when

I put on these silly socks, walk to this diner, and order eggs.
Linda Ronstadt sings while I butter toast.
Poor me. Poor me. Poor poor pitiful me.
The music reminds me how smooth
your small hands felt yesterday, the knuckles
like worry stones in my palm, how I miss you
flailing the pinball machine at Charlie O's
with those wondrous hips, how I've always wanted
to kiss the bruises the cold metal makes;

and then I think of places we might go together
in another lifetime, so I'm writing this note and wearing
these stupid socks that fit perfectly because
I have no other lifetime.

Who's Got the Rada Loa?*

I sold my five-dollar Timex for ten to a Marine Corps private named Richard Johnson. He said his mamma was a mambo priestess and cast a spell shielding him from the demonic rain of shrapnel that would soon kill the best of us. All he had to do was wear it upside down on his right wrist and wind it every midnight. We slipped off base at sunset to run the clubs and bars on Okinawa, our last chance at whores and laughter before Quang Tri. Johnson strutted through the neon streets with square shouldered immortality. His head swayed gently to the rhythm of mamma's three baptized drums and her snake-boned rattle ten thousand miles away, while the copper sound of constant fear dinged inside my ears. Looking for my own protective spirits, I spent his ten on sloe gin and a hooker named Noriko, whose tongue traced the alcohol down my throat and around my navel, heating my blood from the outside in, as if love were an external warmth like mamma's *rada loa*. In the hour that passed, as near as I could tell without my Timex, all of me that was me and all of him that was him flowed from us, pulled by the different vortex of the same spell. I paid Noriko and went to war. Johnson, drunk and mugged for the watch, stumbled from the *Happy Hotel* bar into a back alley, where he bled to death.

*The Rada Loa are the protective guardian powers first saluted in the Voodoo ceremony.

Road Trip

The sun sets
on the Whitehorse Tavern
where we've stopped to drink
a beer with Dylan's drunken ghost.
Lou spies two bangled beauties
clanking arm in arm down Hudson Street
as if it were a fashion runway. She's engrossed
by their closeness. I watch
her nipples harden, jealous for the thrill
of being young, and light a Camel
to keep from kissing her.

Outside the tavern, a bearded man
shadowboxes a birch tree and fades
into the gray smog that falls
from hi-rise hotels, the tumbling dynamo
of pounding blood and electric current
that shrouds Manhattan like a sheet
of wet waxed paper. We disappear
by becoming part of traffic

and drive to the Catskills
cross-hatched with pine trees
and stars so clear I can see through the sky.
Lou's bare and beautiful legs stretch
beneath the dash. She's rocked to sleep
by the low hum of rubber on asphalt
and night folding over the green glow
of the radio like a spent squeezebox.
Janis Joplin grinds out prophecy—
take another little piece of my heart, oh baby
if it makes you feel good—

In three more hours
this road trip will end
as some college opens its doors
and I lose myself in a disjointed myth
that life is "organic" poetry.
All the while, the real myth sleeps
beside me, lips slightly parted.
A loose strand of black hair
slips across her Cuban cheek
and I reach to brush it back,
one last chance at one more trip...
I brush her breast instead.

Steering the Camaro,
my hand is numb, my mind barely conscious
that while Lou loves
boyish charm, it's only sweaty danger
that might get her pants down
like the blind butcher we saw levitate
roast beef across a slicing blade yesterday
with the grace of a seer in his fingers.
I want his power, if only for an instant.
I want to slide across the car and stroke
my friend so gently that her own
moaning wakes her.
I could have done it
twenty years ago before the weight and spread
of age diffused my senses and made love
an intellectual exercise too complex
to simply squeeze and let go.

Sock-hop Serenade

"Oh I was so much older then
I'm younger than that now."
— Bob Dylan

Today as I walked through the alleyways of time
behind Lowell School, past grapevines
where I played Tarzan forty years ago, crossed
Sand Creek bridge in daylight, heard the water tinkle
over stones and into dusk like a right-handed
boogie woogie piano run on a roadhouse Saturday night,
Faye hid there, a faint shadow of memory beneath the bridge,
promising *things* to me for a few sips from a pint
bottle of Mogan David 20/20 hidden in my gym locker.
I didn't know what *things* were until she moistened
the tip of my newly lit Swisher Sweet with her thick lips
and said, "Whatever happens, don't tell Kenny."

Inside the school white socks slipped and slid
across the gym floor, buffing the varnished wood
to the beat of Berry Gordy and whine of Sam Cooke.
Fifty girls swirled and bounced while fifty boys, lining
the long cement wall, shifted from foot to foot
as if dodging the collective smell of Clearasil and Brut.
The art teacher, Miss Hall, smiled at me, arched
her back, and stretched her perfect breasts against her black
sweater. The nipples made me dream about being
a hunger that she might dream about.
Beneath paper streamers and black-light posters
Faye's small hands replaced the neck
of a *Louisville Slugger* in my sweaty palms
and we danced, not just the Twist, the Mashed Potato,
the Swim, and the Bristol Stomp, something greater,
more intricate than the footwork, wilder than the 2-4
drumbeat. We danced till we became the dance,
as if the rhythm remolded us

into strange new creatures whose only desire
was to feel the blood boil and rise in our veins, then fade
as Mr. Sparks changed the records
and the street lamps flashed, lighting the alley,
where I would hike slowly home alone.

The Ballgame

A rain delay, but the field drained well.
Around third base our coach burned
some old rubber tires to dry the puddles.
Black smoke rose as if the diamond
were an altar of burning joss sticks
honoring those among us
who would later be dead.

We lost the game.
We never got our rhythm back.
Maybe we had panicked
when the small twister tossed
the grandstand roof across the parking lot,
as if an angry God had thrown it
because it shielded us from the wet wind.

Two college scouts watched me play second base.
I batted lead-off and "Pumkin" Lambert
threw a slider that ducked in and snapped my left thumb,
like one of those number 2 pencils Mr. Jones broke
in math class while mumbling
about his wife and the gym teacher.
My father pulled me aside and said,
"Deal with the pain. The scouts are watching.
 Spit and throw a little dirt on it. That's what men do."
I did and got the scholarship when the swelling went down.
A year later it disappeared in a flurry
of keg parties, sorority panties, and enlistment papers.
It kept disappearing when I broke
my mind in Vietnam: unheated C-rations on night ambush,
                 the whistle of a single mortar shell,
                 a young girl on her back in a bunker,
                 the stare of her father as he counted the cash,
                 homemade rice wine and Thai sticks,

the giggle of a stoned lieutenant,
napalm at sunrise and the catharsis of friendly fire,
the landing zone at Khe Sahn, and the smell
of smoking flesh rising from running children.
Now my *mind* moves like "Pumkin's" slider. *Semper Fidelis.*
And Dad's advice still saves me.

The Garden
(for my wife, Debbie)

Remember ours?

How we turned the earth over, rubbed the sore soil
with a poultice of eggshells and Miracle Gro
as if it were our stung and fevered child. We covered
seeds, hoed unwanted weeds, exorcised crows
and rabbits in a strange ritual of dance and song.
Until that summer, our neighbors never heard
Appalachian Spring played on pots and pans
by tattooed drunks twirling spoons.

When the corn grew straight and the staked tomatoes
rounded with red life and the squash leaked upward,
our laughter sprayed them all with light. There was no sadness,
only the salmon color of sunrise and a frenzied desire
to wade barefoot in the dew.

Remember the storm?

Around here hog farmers, grain haulers, and old women
still call these small twisters *Fingers of God* because
even a slight touch drives shafts of straw into oak trees
like ten penny nails, houses explode, trains
writhe like garter snakes, airborne. People become memories,
like my father's sister, buried beneath joists, broken beams
and the expectations of her parents.

You cried for hours over the tangled stalks and shattered vines,
cursed all gods for having fingers that would reach down
and rip a dream from someone sustained by little else,
then rented a small plow and returned the earth to a black void
till spring and your strength came again. I laughed
and bought fresh produce at Conway's Market, not grasping,
that our garden was never about the crop.

66

A Fisherman's Grace

The only time my Uncle Jim lost
his temper he had just set down
his new tackle and lit
a Camel. A big snapping turtle
took the bait, the rod, the reel,
and all his composure, to the bottom.

The turtle never surfaced that day
but in the boat a sweat bee stung
me on the finger. I yelled
fuck for the first glorious time
just after my ears hooked
that word when it broke water, leaping
from Jim's lips—*Fuck, fuck,*
oh fuck—as he chased his sinking
tackle through the cattails
and then waded back to shore like King Richard
the Third, a wet and winded shadow
in the sunset. Jim never spoke while he drove us home.

That night on the front porch, he danced by himself
as Benny Goodman's clarinet coaxed
Blue Rhapsody out of the radio, and drank bourbon,
a whole quart. The more I watched him
the more the jazz came alive through
him, the notes got their melody
from the whisper of his shoes across the wooden floor.

When he finally passed out drunk
my mother laid gold cufflinks and a red tie
with his white shirt and blue Brooks Brothers suit.
"Your uncle would rather die than look badly
dressed for the doctors in the morning," she said.

A fisherman's grace
hung like a hospital sheet
over his black lungs while I helped her pack
his shaving cream, his silk pajamas,
his Bass trophy, his morphine pills,
and waited.

At The Museum of Modern Art
In New York City I Wondered:

Suppose Van Gogh shot himself
in the foot with a rifle, rather than sliced
his ear with a carving knife? Would he be
an artist, or just my friend Williams,
who listed left and limped?

Williams doesn't know Van Gogh,
unless that was the name of the opium dealer we found
on a back street in Saigon.
Maybe there's no difference between these men.
They both had beards, red hair, and strange visions
of a world gone mad.
Their shades of blue and hues of red swirled
in paranoid pools of color.
Williams drew graffiti on the concrete walls in Hue,
sold his watch for a blow job in Phu Bai,
laughed as nuoc mam ran over his chin like barbeque sauce,
sobbed when the amphetamines were gone,
placed the barrel of an M-16 against his own foot
and squeezed carefully, as if the trigger would bruise his finger.

After the medics carried him away,
I saw Williams one last time
at Leavenworth Prison,
where the Army sends self-inflicting soldiers.
I visited on a Sunday. He never spoke,
but like this self-portrait of Van Gogh,
stared wildly over my head, as though afraid
of closing his eyes.

On Halloween My Mid-Life Crisis Appears

(for Jack Myers)

I just want a way to grow old gracelessly.
My wife thinks I've gone insane,
drinking gin with no tonic, writing poems
that terrify small children and driving
a purple sports car called The Bitch Goddess.

Though my lungs wheeze as I walk up steps,
I play tennis with my son, dance to the Cajun
Zydeco, drool when girls stroll by, and believe
I can describe the sound of my high mileage body,
an idling engine with worn bearings.
I took a course at college last semester called
Nature or Nurture and touched my anima
by watching Oprah with my daughter.

Tonight, I listen while bunny rabbits,
bumblebees, and a witch knock on the door
and beg my wife for anything with sugar-coating
as if candy might sweeten the sour taste
of passing time, a taste they won't even notice
till the weight of fifty-plus Halloweens presses
on each little belly and pushes
half-digested dreams up into the throat.

My friend Jack just had a triple by-pass.
He's healing and sneaking cigarettes,
hoping I'll feel so sorry for him
and let him win our next game of billiards.
The quest for immortality has no shame.

Maybe he thinks I love him as mentor,
that I recall those long discussions about seeing
the eternal in the ephemeral and reptilian brains
capable of love, the musical pulse of language
and how it drives the mentally ill
into the streets, or how the anima wails
at its own loss while the animus slides headlong
down the neck of a bourbon bottle.

No, he knows why I love him. He knows because
he's finally crossed over that singular vacuum
existing between time and space
in all men, that darkness appearing slowly
in the mind, as if lights were being turned
off one room at a time in a cheap hotel.
I love him because he used to drive
a taxi cab and wait for words to pay
the fare and now, he doesn't bother.

When I rack those balls and he breaks
for our next game, I won't *let* him win.
He just *will.* He'll laugh and watch me struggle
with the game he's already mastered.

Thirty Years from the TET Offensive

A car crashes and the Life Flight helicopter swoops so low
over the tree line, its black shadow clips the back of my head.
When I hear those turbines whine and rotors slap air
   with a rhythmic thud,
then Jim Morrison chants, "this is the end, beautiful end my friend…",
then my left knee aches for whiskey to dull the pain,
then I'm forced to drink beer warm, and eat powdered eggs cold,
then rain pours gray for several days, and those days fall down like rain,
then I can't sleep because someone pops the tab top on a Pepsi can,
slides a deadbolt home in the dark, bumps my bad leg,
   or steps behind me;
then summer sours the river, cypress molds and I smell fish rotting,
then the wind screams, the sky explodes, bone sears into red powder,
air fills my lungs like bits of broken glass, and those already dead
continue dying, charred slivers of wood and stone. Hell, thirty years
later I'm still hiding, nauseous and naked, in the napalmed jungle.

Running the Voodoo Down

My clock radio blasts
me into dawn.
I see the flick of a wrist
outside my window
and the morning news lands
between the sidewalk and a step.
The boy rides on
singing no song loudly
as I retrieve the paper, an unshaven dog
in slippers and oversized robe.
Sandy the nurse jogs by, waves
disapprovingly at my first cigarette.
The only conscious drunk in town
bends, scoops cans from the curb
across the street and places them
into a plastic bag, hoping
to recycle them into bottles
of Wild Irish Rose by sunset.
Southern Railway cattle cars
whistle through the crossing
like empty martini glasses clacking
and I am alone in the middle of nothing,
the center of everything.

I open the newspaper.
Swarms of small words buzz
into the gray light like bees
escaping the hive.
I let them go to watch Mrs. Martin
slowly drive toward the drugstore.
Her left front tire, out of balance
since Mr. Martin died of cancer,
flaps on wet asphalt : thump-hiss
What if... What if... What if...

What if
the spent bullet that struck my chest
beneath an open flack jacket
thirty years ago isn't spent,
is killing me slowly?
What if it had been fired from point blank range,
a bolt from a god in black pajamas?
What if what I had slapped and caught with an open hand
was the hole it left, if my blood had congealed to paste,
and my lungs lost their vacuum?
What if the last things I saw were lines
on my best friend's right palm closing my eyes?

A horn blows.
My neighbor ushers his sullen child
up the steps of a yellow school bus.
"Morning Jim. What's doing?"
"Reading the paper."
But what I'm doing is
glancing at pink flowers on white cotton underwear
pressed against the storm door across the street
as Marcy lets her bulldog out to pee.
My eyes fold an oak tree into the cloudless sky.
I frisk my pockets for egg money,
listen to a hum inside the daylight lifting fog.
It sounds like stardust weeping.
Darkness ends around me the way my father
would have ended it, with a pledge
that all things dim grow progressively brighter.
He always saw the new day
as something more than it really was.
Yesterday the coroner, who reeked
of talcum powder and isopropyl,
lifted retinas, one good iris, even aqueous humor
from my father's face. Someone else will get his eyes
but he willed his sight to me.

I change my clothes
and on my morning walk, pass a vacant house
on Hart Street remembering
this same doorway Christmas morning, 1955.
Our gold Plymouth stops
curbside and Dad leaves a turkey
and three small toys on the porch.
I watch his lips move—*all you get from life
is what you give to others*—but the sound
of his voice is swallowed by my sobs.
I thought the toys were mine.

Out of breath
I stop at unconscious attention
on a square of dying grass at the courthouse lawn.
A sculptured eagle on a stone spike carries names
skyward … Isiah Beadles, Isaac Decker, Josiah Palmer …
the weathered letters shine, faint window lights
far across a cold lake.
The 58th Indiana Volunteers built this marker
in 1865, a cenotaph for the living.
Is memory prophecy? These letters, scrambled,
reappeared a hundred years later, on dog tags
10,000 miles away smelling
of cordite and gunpowder. The groans
erupting from the black ground, the hunger
for silence—all the same.
Once, before a ballgame, I found four combat medals
buried beneath argyle socks in an old trunk.
I remember Dad snatching them from my hand
as if they were burning matches.
"The sins of the fathers…", he whispered.
The same ceramic guilt that glazed his proud eyes
coated them again when I was carried home a hero
and broken from Vietnam, like a cheap watch
that keeps losing time.

I cross the street and enter
Cody's Diner. Eggs fry, bacon splatters,
warm coffee seeps from a worn auto-drip.
Racing forms crackle in calloused hands.
The smoke from seven cigarettes crawls upward
like cobwebs on the grease stained wall.
The corner stool is covered with a funeral
wreath of freshly cut flowers.
No one tries to make "sorry your dad died"
sound sincere with breakfast.

Back home after breakfast an angel falls.
I catch him by his wings, and when I open my hand,
a moth escapes.
Blue-haired women
carry crock pots stuffed with ham and pie tins
crusted with cooked apples to my front door.
Like my father, their vision of life seems nourished
by their attention to death.
The street sings a dirge that only I hear
in the wail of a small terrier tied to a fence post.

My father once drank a fifth of Beefeater's gin,
drove to the city pound and, crying, clipped
the chain off the gate.
While he locked himself
inside the bottle, forty dogs ran free.
By noon, I begin searching
the same bottle for the key
he dropped in there.
The bottle empties at dusk. I disappear
by becoming part
of the neighborhood around me.

Gray men drive home from work,
schoolgirls hopscotch,
skipping over scarred concrete.
None of them know how close to death
this day brought them. What would they
change and why would they change it,
even if they did?

The neighbor's son leans into their magnolia bush,
kissing white blossoms, but I'm the one caressed
by the boughs, carried by fragrance into a softer world,
where Holloway suckers last all day,
where bicycle lock chains lie unused in an open garage,
where deadbolts exist in science fiction books
and the smell of leather ball gloves and Neat's foot oil
mixes easily with the taste of my gin…

I begin to see in this boy's blameless smile
the reason to go on my father saw in mine.

A phone rings.
Someone calls a dog home.
A cat in heat squeals.
I fall asleep for the first time
with no link to my own beginning,
with no fear of my own end.

Awakened at midnight
on the same front porch where I began,
I hear the hum of cicadas
as the flow of waterfalls.
Starlings and sparrows sing with larger voices
songs of a smaller realm.
On the arm of the porch swing a pregnant mantis
steps cautiously toward space. She can't fly
and has eaten the father of her children.

Overhead the sky is so clear
I can see through the stars, each one
a window into some long hidden attic,
holding my father's ashes and his light.
An attic much like the one across the street
where a new father nails sheetrock
beneath a bare light bulb, each hammer blow
a shout against the darkness, each panel hung
a larger world for his newly born child.

Snapshots

"I wish I were a camera. I wish it all the time.
My eyes would have a reason, my life would have a rhyme."
— David Crosby

1 – 1/5/56

How big Aunt Betty's belly
looked when I was eight years old,
how she cried and vomited every morning
for months, even after Doc Peck said,
"There's nothing there but hysteria."
Still, my mother held a cold cloth
to her sister's forehead with one hand,
pretending to feel the baby move with the other.

2 – 1/5/67

Monsoons shot raindrops bigger
than bullets. They strafed my helmet,
a symphony of sameness, a hypnotic
splattered mist that never lifted.
In the bunker I dreamt dry dreams
of Saigon streets—the sway
of rickshaws, rattle of palm trees,
the rustle of silk, the adrenaline
tingling in a French whore,
and defeated the desire to lie face down
in the bright yellow mud, just one more
casualty of a constant dull thud.

3 – 1/5/68

My fireteam eased by a thatch hut, palms sweating,
safeties off, frightened boys on a first dance
with the dying. A widow squatted in the webbed shadows
and picked through a child's matted hair. Her fingers
pulled lice from the scalp. She bit the heads off, one at a time,
while I imagined my body twitching between uneven teeth,
tumbling through betel juice and drool to the dead ground.
That night, alone in my bunker, away from her eyes, I stared
as orange and blue flames from a smudge pot waltzed black
shadows across the sandbags. Even in the uncertain light,
I never lost my focus as a soldier. Even in the soft rustle
of diesel smoke, I never cared why she was a widow.

4 – 1/5/78

Today, four sparrows flew as one bird
from a black bridge railing on the Wabash River.
A fisherman floating beneath me unfolded
his nylon net, feeding the caramel water dreams
of a big catch, while the wind brayed at his back.
He stood in the bow swaying like an unsteady drunk
on an uneven dance floor and waved as if we were
friends. As if we were friends, I waved back.

5 – 1/5/88

My cup left a ring of spilled coffee
on the table. Each time I drank and returned
the cup, the circle became less whole,
rearranged constantly by pressure from a source
it could not recognize. On my plate, two
poached eggs stared upward. I felt the increasing weight
of unbuttered toast in my hand and the slight flutter
of a sparrow's wing in my chest.

6 – 1/5/90

Everything was white, except the blood
and my son's ceramic eyes. How big they looked
for an eight year old, like blueberries
in small bowls of milk. Outside the window,
beyond the smell of isopropyl, white snow
strangled the frightened trees. John's surgeon said,
"The tumor's gone, we think. Nothing but air now."
I held a cold cloth to my son's forehead with one hand,
pretending to feel the empty space with the other.

7 – 1/5/2000

From the top of the Farm Bureau Co-op
grain elevator, I see the dead tree
in the yielding meadow beyond Lynch Road
where Mike pissed twice on prom night before
lightning split the wood and chased
us along the ground, as if it were a hot yellow stream the sky
pissed back. Mike outran that lightning
till it caught him on a jungle trail outside Phu Bai.
I'm still running.